NEW ZEALAND
the essential landscape

For my daughters
Francesca, Lily and Zara

NEW ZEALAND
the essential landscape

Rob Brown

craig potton publishing

First published in 2011 by Craig Potton Publishing
98 Vickerman Street, PO Box 555, Nelson, New Zealand
www.craigpotton.co.nz

© Text and photography: Rob Brown

ISBN 978 1 877517 45 7

Design: Robbie Burton
Scanning by Tradescans, Rangiora, New Zealand
Printed in China by Midas Printing International Ltd

Contents

The West Coast

Most of the West Coast landscape is wild mountainous terrain that includes the western side of the Southern Alps; a magnificent landscape of glaciated mountains, big rivers, dense forests and rugged valleys stretching 450 kilometres from Victoria Forest Park in the north to the Cascade River in the south. No other region on mainland New Zealand has such a high percentage of its landscape protected as either national parks or conservation areas, or such a high percentage of the original landscape still in a natural condition.

Formed over millions of years by the Pacific plate moving west into the Australian plate, and this in turn crunching into the former and sliding northeast up the Alpine Fault, the mountains of the West Coast dominate almost everything about this province. Very few high mountain ranges in the world are in such close proximity to the sea as the Southern Alps and this affects everything from the rainfall and climate, to the dense mantle of rainforest that covers much of the region.

Wherever you are on the West Coast, wild nature seems to be on your backdoor, although this can disguise the very rich human history of 'the Coast'. Much of this human history has its basis in a rugged pioneer spirit developed around the non-renewable industries of logging and mining. The population of the West Coast has ebbed and flowed, depending on where these industries found resources to extract. Formerly bustling gold and timber towns like Kumara and Hari Hari are now shadows of their former selves, while other settlements like Franz Josef have grown rapidly with tourism over recent decades.

This social history still influences the West Coast today. Despite the obvious natural beauty of the West Coast, there remains a tension between conservation of that beauty and the further commercial exploitation of

Coastline beside the Heaphy Track, Kahurangi National Park

the landscape. These divergent views have led to many confrontations in the last 30 years between those trying to preserve the natural world and those who believe the future of the West Coast economy depends on a continuation of extractive industries, albeit with a more modern nod to conservation concerns.

In recent years the West Coast has looked towards less-extractive industries as the way of the future. Tourism is now a mainstay of the economy, while dairy farming, although not without its impacts, also plays an important role in the lowland rural areas.

Wet weather is an integral part of the West Coast experience. All of the West Coast is exposed to the prevailing westerly weather that collides with the mountains releasing large amounts of precipitation in the form of rain and snow. The wettest recorded place in New Zealand is actually the Cropp River in the ranges inland from Hokitika. It is not unusual for the Cropp to record between 9 and 11 metres of rainfall in a calendar year, and it holds the New Zealand record for a 365-day period: 16 metres.

Higher up, precipitation falls as snow and collects on both large and small néves that feed numerous glaciers on the western side of the Alps. Two of the largest and more accessible glaciers are at Fox and Franz Josef. Both of these glaciers descend 2,000 metres from the high mountains into temperate rainforest and terminate at an altitude of just 250 metres above sea level. Winter often brings the most settled weather and if the eastern plains of Canterbury are freezing under southerly winds, the Coast will often have an outstanding crisp, clear day with the mountains sparkling under a fall of fresh snow.

WESTLAND/TAI POUTINI NATIONAL PARK

The diversity of landscape on the West Coast is perhaps nowhere more apparent than in the Coast's first national park – Westland – that covers some 127,650 hectares from New Zealand's highest mountain down through to the sea just 23 kilometres away from these highest summits.

The beauty of the Franz Josef and Fox Glaciers has attracted tourists for over 100 years and the earliest scenic reserves were set aside protecting the two valleys in 1911. In the late 1950s there was resistance to 'locking up' the land on the

Coastline near Kohaihai, Karamea

West Coast in a national park, but the mood changed after a proposal arose to extend Mt Cook National Park over into the western néves. Parochialism, alive and well on the Coast, was not going to let a Canterbury park board extend its control over the main divide and in 1960 a new Westland National Park suddenly had many supporters. Although modest at first, the park has steadily grown with such additions as the Karangarua Valley, lowland forests from Okarito south to Gillespies Beach and, more recently, the forests around Saltwater Lagoon.

In 1990 Westland National Park, along with all other protected public lands in South Westland and Mt Cook, as well as Mt Aspiring and Fiordland National Parks, were accorded World Heritage status as the Te Wahipounamu World Heritage Area. This recognition was the culmination of an environmental struggle to protect the tall podocarp forests south of the Cook River from logging. A decade later, the last government logging of indigenous forest came to an end, protecting all of the West Coast's remaining primeval old growth forests in Crown or public ownership. In its suite of mountains-to-sea landforms, Westland National Park provides a fitting gateway to what is one of the last great tracts of wilderness terrain left in the temperate regions of the world.

PAPAROA NATIONAL PARK

The creation of Paparoa National Park in 1987 again highlighted the tension between preservation and a utilitarian view of the landscape. Paparoa National Park protects one of the few remaining lowland areas of forest left in the northern West Coast and this forest cloaks a complex limestone landscape full of caves, sinkholes, sculptured limestone streams and gorges.

The coastal road gives just a glimpse of the complexity and ruggedness that is hidden in the hills beyond. The opportunities to explore the Paparoas range from the very easy, such as those at the famous Pancake Rocks at Dolomite Point, to the remote wilderness area of the main range. A highlight of the park is the tracks through the coastal limestone canyons and the Inland Pack Track offers a good walking opportunity at a more moderate level along an historic route that was used before the coastal road opened in 1927.

The original proposal for this national park

was nearly three times the size and covered most of the Paparoa Range. This was gradually whittled away as various mining and local interests lobbied the government down to protecting just 30,000 hectares.

In 2004 much of the remaining Paparoa Range was gazetted as a Wilderness Area that affords a level of protection designed to keep it as natural as possible, without even the intrusion of huts and tracks. The tops of the Paparoa Range are similar in their geology to parts of Fiordland, a result of this part of New Zealand having been shunted 480 kilometres northwards over millions of years along the Alpine Fault.

KAHURANGI NATIONAL PARK

North of Westport a lonely road heads to the hidden wonderland of Karamea, the spectacular coastal section of the Heaphy Track and the Oparara limestone arches. Many of the wild places in this part of New Zealand were incorporated into Kahurangi National Park in 1996, the country's second largest at 452,889 hectares.

In the mid-1960s the former New Zealand Forest Service responded to a community request to establish protection for the area by creating North-west Nelson Forest Park. The NZFS worked hard to reopen historic tracks in the area like the Heaphy and Wangapeka, and established a large network of huts and tracks in other parts. But the conservation and recreation goals of the Forest Service conflicted with its mandate to supply timber and some ill-advised forestry experiments around Karamea would set the scene for the forest park to be later raised to the status of national park.

The Tasman Wilderness Area north of the Karamea River and the coastline north of the Heaphy River to Kahurangi Point are two of the outstanding wild places protected within Kahurangi National Park.

FOLLOWING PAGE Moria Gate Arch, Oparara River, Kahurangi National Park

Mt Euclid, Paparoa Wilderness Area

Pororari River, Paparoa National Park

Paparoa coastline south of Truman Track, Paparoa National Park

Approaching southwesterly storm, Dolomite Point, Paparoa National Park
OPPOSITE Evening light, Dolomite Point, Paparoa National Park
FOLLOWING PAGE Lake Mahinepua and the Southern Alps near Hokitika

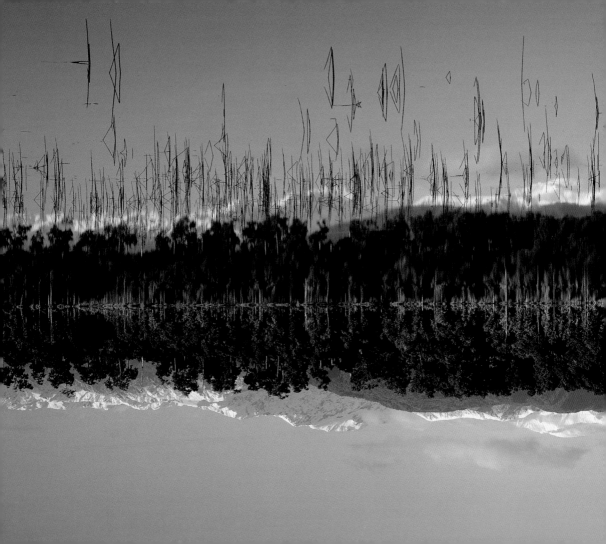

Lake Mapourika, Westland/Tai Poutini National Park
OPPOSITE Winter sunrise, Lake Matheson, Westland/Tai Poutini National Park

Fox Glacier, Westland/Tai Poutini National Park PREVIOUS PAGE Farmland near Fox Glacier
below a backdrop of Aoraki/Mt Cook and Mt La Perouse (centre)

Franz Josef Glacier, Westland/Tai Poutini National Park

Coastal rimu forest, Bruce Bay, South Westland   PREVIOUS PAGE Moonrise over Mt Tasman (left) and Aoraki/Mt Cook from Gillespies Beach, Westland/Tai Poutini National Park

Driftwood near the mouth of the Cook River, South Westland

Fiordland and Stewart Island

FIORDLAND NATIONAL PARK

Author Douglas Adams described the visual splendour of Fiordland in his book *Last Chance to See* as: 'one of the most astounding pieces of land anywhere on God's earth' and went on to add that 'one's first impulse, standing on a cliff top surveying it all, is simply to burst into spontaneous applause'. He was not overstating the case.

More superlatives have been used to describe Fiordland than any other place in New Zealand. The bare facts give an indication why the area so frequently evokes extravagant description: it is almost all contained within what is far and away New Zealand's largest national park (1,260,708 hectares); and within this park are New Zealand's two largest wilderness areas, six major glaciated lakes along its eastern side, at least 15 major fiords on the western seaward side and innumerable unnamed mountains, valleys, rivers, streams and other prominent landscape features.

One of the earliest champions of protecting this magnificent tract of wilderness was Dunedin politician Thomas Mackenzie, who had extensively explored Fiordland on several arduous trips. As early as 1894, Mackenzie proposed national park status for Fiordland, and, largely as a result of his efforts, a huge area of 800,000 hectares was set aside in 1904 for future 'national park purposes'. Nothing remotely resembling this scale had previously been protected for scenic and conservation purposes in New Zealand and this area later formed the core of the 1952 national park.

Much of Fiordland's grandeur is a result of the irresistible force of ice-age glaciers carving out this landscape from solid rock over much of the past two million years. When the ice finally retreated at the end of the last glacial maximum, some 12,000 years ago, it left behind a stunning landscape of fiords, mountains and lakes.

The other main factor in the shaping of

The Darran Mountains from Key Summit, Routeburn Track, Fiordland National Park

Fiordland is the characteristics of its parent rocks. In striking contrast to the Southern Alps, virtually the entire region is composed of hard, crystalline igneous (granite, gabbro and diorite) and metamorphic (mainly gneiss) rocks. This has meant that the landscape largely held its shape after the ice-age glaciers retreated and accounts for the steep-sided U-shaped valleys, fiords and sharp peaks that are such a feature of the Fiordland landscape.

The most accessible way to experience Fiordland National Park is to drive the magnificent scenic highway from Te Anau to Milford Sound. Even here, despite the often constant tourist traffic, it is possible to step off the road onto a secluded forest track and feel yourself lost in the immensity of Fiordland. Easy short walks into forest and alpine grandeur are available all along this road, while for those looking for something a little more challenging, day walks up into the Lake Marian basin, to Key Summit and to Gertrude Saddle provide the chance to venture more deeply into some of the most chiselled and spectacular of Fiordland's landscapes.

Fiordland boasts three of New Zealand's Great Walks – the Kepler, Routeburn and Milford tracks. Of these, the Milford Track has the longest and most interesting history. In the early 1900s English writer and suffragette Blanche Baughan walked the track and described it glowingly in a London journal as 'the finest walk in the world'. While this was simply a felicitous marketing slogan, there is no doubt the Milford remains a very fine walk, one that exemplifies all the qualities that together make Fiordland distinctive: lush rainforests, waterfalls, U-shaped valleys, spectacular mountains and, almost inevitably, rain – the Milford area is doused with up to nine metres of rainfall every year.

The track was first opened in the late 1880s and for many years the only way to 'legally' walk the track was through the government owned Tourist Hotel Corporation (THC). When the boundaries of Fiordland National Park were drawn up the track was logically included. However the Park Board resisted pressure to provide for independent trampers of a more modest means. By the 1960s many local trampers had become frustrated with this situation and in Easter 1965 the Otago

Key Summit, Routeburn Track, Fiordland National Park

Tramping Club staged a protest 'Freedom Walk' over the track. The Board relented and agreed to erect three separate huts for use by independent trampers that are still in use today.

In the 1960s and early 1970s, Fiordland became the scene of one of New Zealand's most significant environmental battles. This was a pivotal event in the nation's history and marked a turning point in how New Zealanders viewed both their most cherished wild landscapes and the protection given to them through national park status.

In the 1950s the Electricity Department had begun investigating the possibility of raising Lake Manapouri's level by up to 30 metres as part of a hydroelectric scheme to provide power to a proposed aluminium smelter at Bluff. The drilling of tunnels for the scheme began in 1964 after a catalogue of bungled government negotiations and legislative manoeuvring designed to override the National Parks Act – all of which set the government on a collision course with public opinion.

By the early 1970s, as the scheme neared completion, feelings were running so high that a petition was signed by 265,000 New Zealanders.

With a looming election, Labour reversed its earlier support of the project and promised that the level of the lake would not be raised. The National government on the other hand continued to drag its heels and subsequently lost the 1972 election. One of Labour's first acts in government was to preserve the lake's level by setting up the Guardians of Lake Manapouri which would have statutory authority over monitoring the lake level and ensuring the power scheme kept the lake within its natural limits. It was a major victory for people, united from all walks of life, who believed that Fiordland's beauty and ecology had clear priority over industry.

STEWART ISLAND/RAKIURA

Around 83 per cent of Stewart Island is protected as national park and, except for the village of Oban, native vegetation covers the entire island.

That Stewart Island has survived with its natural ecosystems largely intact is as much chance as design. At various times since European settlement, attempts have been made to make the island more 'productive'. Early ventures in sealing and whaling followed the animals they slaughtered into oblivion. A ship building settlement in Port Pegasus, set up by a duplicitous seller of the New Zealand dream, subsequently failed, as did the tin mining and saw-milling ventures. In 1908 the government ironically contracted a well-known conservationist – Dr Leonard Cockayne – to investigate the island's suitability for farming, but his resulting report provided instead a passionate argument for conservation. As his often quoted summary stated:

> 'And this brings me to that feature which gives the island its special and perhaps someday unique value. The face of the earth is changing so rapidly that soon, in temperate regions at any rate, there will be little of primitive Nature left. In the Old World it is practically gone forever. Here, then, is Stewart Island's prime advantage, and one hard to overestimate. It is an actual piece of the primeval world.'

In 2002 this vision was finally given the recognition it deserved when the various reserves and stewardship lands on the island were collected together to form Rakiura National Park. As a consequence, many come today to enjoy the wilds of Stewart Island, whether to wander among the extensive sand dunes of Mason Bay, or to tramp the wild western beaches of the North-west Circuit Track, or to explore the southern wilderness of Port Pegasus, or just to enjoy the simple pleasures of bird-watching in and around Halfmoon Bay.

Rakiura is also one of the few accessible places in New Zealand where you can regularly hear a full-throated morning chorus; a fortunate consequence of the fact that Stewart Island has so far escaped the stoat invasion which has so devastated birdlife on mainland New Zealand. And the island is of course rightly celebrated as being the only place where we can see our national icon – the kiwi – wandering around in the daytime – an experience that is likely to warm even the hardest of hearts.

FOLLOWING PAGE Lake Adelaide with Mt Sabre (left of centre), Darran Mountains, Fiordland National Park

Emily Peak from Lake Mackenzie, Routeburn Track, Fiordland National Park
OPPOSITE Ailsa Mountains and Lake Mackenzie, Routeburn Track, Fiordland National Park

Clinton River, Milford Track, Fiordland National Park

Mt Elliot from Mackinnon Pass, Milford Track, Fiordland National Park

Mountain daisies and Mt Talbot, Hollyford Valley, Fiordland National Park

Last of the evening light behind Mitre Peak, Milford Sound, Fiordland National Park

Alpine tussock lands above Green Lake, Fiordland National Park

Ridgeline above Lake Ronald, Fiordland National Park

Port Pegasus from Bald Cone, Rakiura National Park, Stewart Island

Evening light, Mason Bay sand dunes, Rakiura National Park, Stewart Island

West Ruggedy Beach, Rakiura National Park, Stewart Island

Kiwi tracks, Mason Bay, Rakiura National Park, Stewart Island

Rata forest near Hellfire Pass, Rakiura National Park, Stewart Island

Christmas Village Beach, North-west Circuit Track, Rakiura National Park, Stewart Island

Otago and the Catlins

The hinterland of the Otago landscape contrasts markedly from much of the rest of the South Island. This region inherits much of its physical character from the dominant metamorphic rock in the landscape – schist. From the highest peaks of Mt Aspiring National Park, to the dramatic backdrop to Queenstown of the Remarkables, to the strange tors that sit on the high Central Otago peneplain, schist rock, infused with mica, sparkles under the clear New Zealand light.

The other distinctive element of Otago's hinterland is the tall tussocks that cover much of the landscape. The early European settlers recognised the farming potential of this tussock-covered land and within a few short years farmers established large flocks of sheep on the rolling highlands of Central Otago.

One of the largest high-country runs was Morven Hills near Lindis Pass and at one stage sheep numbers on this station alone totalled over 135,000. There are still impressive historic woolsheds dating from the 1870s here and, like many of the farm buildings in Otago, they are built from the readily available schist. Merino sheep continued to be the backbone of the rural economy throughout the twentieth century, albeit with much reduced sheep numbers.

In recent years, recognition has been given to some of these outstanding tussock and tor landscapes with some high-country areas being retired from grazing and protected as conservation parks. One of the more outstanding is the 21,000 hectare Te Papanui Tussocklands Conservation Park covering much of the Lammermoor and Lammerlaw Ranges. Unfortunately much of the sense of space and wildness in this landscape is now threatened by plans by one of the State's energy generation companies to build a huge wind farm near here. While there are some areas in Otago and Southland suitable for wind farms,

Nugget Point Lighthouse, Catlins Coastline

it is the sheer size and scale of this proposal, as well as its visual impact on one of the more beautiful highland areas, that has generated so much opposition.

In 1861 gold was discovered in Gabriel's Gully near Lawrence, signalling the start of a boom time for Otago. It was the first of many gold strikes and wealth flooded into the region. Gold towns sprang up in Queenstown, Arrowtown and Cromwell, which prospered and survived when the gold ran out, while others, like St Bathans and Macetown, struggled on as historical reminders of this bustling time. By the 1870s, on the back of both wool and gold, Dunedin was the richest city in New Zealand and many grand old buildings in the city date from this time. While some have largely been empty since these glory days, Dunedin nonetheless remains a city with many fine Victorian era buildings such as Larnach Castle and the Dunedin Railway Station.

Land use has changed in many rural areas over time. By the 1980s trial plantings of grapes had shown Central Otago's climate and soils were perfect for Pinot grapes. Based around Queenstown and Alexandra, the Central Otago wine industry rapidly expanded in the 1990s and while still small nationally, produces some of the world's finest Pinot Noir wine.

Elsewhere in Otago are a number of easily accessible scenic landscapes. The strange spherical boulders at Moeraki have attracted visitors for over 100 years and further south the Otago Peninsula itself has many enchanting coastal spots far from the madding crowds. The major lakes of Wakatipu, Wanaka and Hawea are focal points for the Central Otago tourism industry and rightly famed for their beauty in all seasons.

MT ASPIRING NATIONAL PARK

The headwaters of Lake Wanaka and Wakatipu lead to one of the most spectacular alpine environments in New Zealand. Mt Aspiring National Park is in many ways one of the most accessible of New Zealand's high alpine regions with the path to the highest mountains often being through wide-open tussock flats surrounded by open beech forests.

The Otago section of the New Zealand Alpine Club began campaigning for a national park around the spectacular glacial horn of Tititea or

Eroded coastal platform near Jacks Bay, Catlins coastline

Mt Aspiring (3,033 metres) as early as the 1930s. Undeniably one of the most beautiful natural areas in New Zealand, it is perhaps surprising that it took until 1964 for this alpine wonderland to become a national park. So unenthusiastic was the government of the day in gazetting the park that at the opening ceremony the Minister of Lands commented that 'this would be New Zealand's last national park'. To date, New Zealand has 14 national parks with Mt Aspiring being the tenth on the list.

Since its creation, Mount Aspiring National Park has been progressively enlarged, particularly on the western side, and has nearly doubled in size to 355,543 hectares. In 1970 the rugged headwaters of the Waiatoto and Arawhata Rivers were added to the park and, after a particularly long campaign, the geologically interesting Red Hills were also included in 1990. In 1996, after a 40-year campaign by the Federated Mountain Clubs, the Red Hills were included in the Olivine Wilderness Area; an area completely free of huts and tracks, which covers nearly one quarter of the park and includes the Olivine Ice Plateau. Wilderness Areas play an important role as the wildest and least-developed part of the spectrum of outdoor experiences in New Zealand. They offer something increasingly rare in the world; a chance to visit nature entirely on nature's terms, without the normal easing of the way provided by facilities such as huts, tracks or bridges.

THE CATLINS

The coastal landscape south of Dunedin is one of the unexpected delights of New Zealand and for many years was considered one of the country's hidden treasures off the main tourist track. In recent years this has changed and few visitors to the South Island now leave the Catlins off their itinerary. On the coastal and lowland parts of the Catlins, little remains of the original native vegetation cover of this unique landscape, but a smattering of scenic reserves provide relaxing opportunities to enjoy nature. Along the coast, the forest has often been cleared all the way to the cliff edge in the last 50 years, but in gullies and steeper terrain inland, particularly on the Maclennan Range, large stands of virgin forest remain.

Catlins Forest Park protects much of the remaining forest and, although somewhat fragmented, these forest blocks nevertheless comprise the largest remaining area of native forest on the eastern side of the South Island. Along the banks of the Catlins River, through one of the bigger blocks, one of the few remaining populations of yellowhead or mohua still survive, largely due to the intensive efforts by the Department of Conservation to trap stoats and rats. This bird's canary-like call is an unmistakable sound in these forests.

Waterfalls are one of the distinctive attractions of the Catlins. Throughout the region a number of popular short walks lead through forest to modest but very pretty cascades. Purakaunui Falls must be one of the more photographed falls in New Zealand but Matai and McLean Falls are also well worth a visit.

Ultimately, though, the coastline lends the Catlins much of their charm and ruggedness. Throughout the Catlins are a series of wild beaches, usually framed at each end with dramatic coastal headlands, and on many of these beaches at the right time of day travellers can reliably see yellow-eyed penguins in the wild, as well as the gruff New Zealand (Hooker's) sea lion.

Towards the southern end of the Catlins at Curio Bay are the petrified remains of the sub-tropical woodland that once covered the region. The fossilised remains here date back 160 million years and the trees share similarities with modern kauri and tropical conifer trees.

Two significant lighthouses at Nugget Point and Waipapa Point mark each end of the Catlins Coast. They signal how treacherous this coast can be and in 1881 the reef at Waipapa Point was the scene of one of New Zealand's worst maritime disasters when the *SS Tararua* foundered. Of the 151 people onboard, only 20 survived.

Lower McLean Falls, Catlins Forest Park

Septarian concretions, Moeraki Boulders Scenic Reserve, Otago

Moonrise over Mt Aspiring/Tititea from Cascade Saddle, Mt Aspiring National Park

West face of Mt Aspiring/Tititea, Mt Aspiring National Park
FOLLOWING PAGE Rippon Vineyard, Lake Wanaka, Central Otago

Stewart Creek Falls near Makarora, Mt Aspiring National Park

Schist canyon near Haast Pass, Mt Aspiring National Park

The Remarkables (left) and the Lake Wakatipu Basin from Coronet Peak, Queenstown

Canterbury

THE PLAINS AND PENINSULA

The Canterbury Plains extend for 240 kilometres from north to south and 70 kilometres from east to west and is by far the most extensive area of flat terrain in New Zealand. The plains have been formed by massive deposition of outwash gravels from the rapidly eroding Southern Alps. Carried largely by ice-age glaciers to the eastern edge of the alps, then constantly spread seawards by the braided rivers that drain across the plains, this powerful geological process has connected the Southern Alps to what had earlier been the offshore volcanic Banks 'Island'.

The plains are just one element of a surprisingly complex Canterbury geology. Running through the western edge of the plains, at the foothills of the Southern Alps, from the Waitaki River in the south all the way to the Kaikoura coastline, is a long band of limestone. This limestone landscape provided several important features for early Maori in the region, including shelter, landmarks and canvasses for recording their world. Scattered throughout this landscape are numerous rock shelters containing ancient Maori art hinting at the early human history of Canterbury; a powerful visual reminder of how different this landscape must have looked and how the pathways through it relied on a deep feel for this geography. Today, in this rolling limestone landscape, roads and fencing annex the geography in a different way and numerous farm buildings dot the valleys and ridges to indicate that it is still a land of fertile provision.

Deforestation in Canterbury came close to total annihilation of native woodlands, leaving it one of the most heavily modified landscapes in New Zealand. Early Maori burned off some tracts of the plains and foothill forest to create grazing area for moa, but beginning in the 1850s the new settlers from Europe went about forest clearance with renewed gusto. Almost all of the great totara trees on Banks Peninsula were cut down for one of the sawmills on the peninsula. The remaining forest was simply burnt down to create grazing land with little thought to the ecological impact.

In the 1860s, Canterbury farmer and ecologist Thomas Potts made a thoughtful plea for conservation, no doubt based on what he saw happening near his home on Banks Peninsula. In his collected writings *Out in the Open,* he wrote:

'In conclusion, let a few words be recorded for the preservation of our native fauna. It is work of difficulty, except with a few, to get folks interested in the subject; amidst the busy swarm of men pressing onward in the struggle for wealth or position... The most striking , not to say alarming, alterations that have rapidly followed the progress of European settlement, in some districts are due to the fact that the conservation of forests is either much disregarded or entirely ignored.'

Today most of the remaining forests have been protected, thanks largely to the pioneering conservation efforts of Potts and his successors. The contemporary conservation issue is water, something that we've always taken largely for granted in Canterbury. Four great river systems – the Waitaki, Rakaia, Rangitata and Waimakariri – as well as numerous other significant waterways, drain out of the mountain catchments onto the plains. The rivers of Canterbury are some of the finest examples of braided river ecosystems anywhere in the world; the sort of landscape found on this scale in only a small number of places like Alaska, Argentina, Iceland and Tibet.

On the eastern edge of the plain, at the connection with Bank's Peninsula, is Christchurch, the South Island's largest city. The city is immeasurably a better place to live in because Harry Ell, one of Potts' conservation successors, fought long and hard to ensure the Port Hills, which provide a backdrop to the city, were protected for all to enjoy. The tracks, reserves and tea-houses (like Sign of the Kiwi) were all part of his grand vision to build a walking track between Christchurch and Akaroa; a project he almost singlehandedly willed into being between the 1890s and 1920s.

In many ways the public conservation ideals of people like Ell were a natural extension of wanting to 'build a better world'. The early European settlers, many of whom were searching for some sort of Arcadian rural community, and a chance to escape the over-population of Great Britain, embraced this idea of a new 'Britain of the South'.

Christchurch was originally a planned 'New Zealand Company' settlement and 792 'Canterbury Pilgrims' unloaded from four ships at Lyttelton in 1850. They trudged over the Bridle Path to their new town that had already been planned and named by the Canterbury Association two years previously. The city still bears the hallmarks of that Arcadian dream today with its neatly ordered streets around a central square, its large central park (Hagley Park) and in the centre of it all the Anglican Cathedral (although sadly the magnificent renaissance style Catholic Basilica was built later a kilometre away off the main square).

On February 22nd 2011 much of the history of Christchurch came crashing down when a shallow magnitude 6.3 earthquake struck at 12.51 p.m. This earthquake followed a stronger deeper one centred out on the plains in September 2010 that had already weakened many of the city's largest buildings. One hundred and eighty one people died in the latter quake and many of the city's heritage buildings were severely damaged, most beyond repair. It was a reminder that while nature has blessed Canterbury with some outstanding natural beauty, like all of New Zealand, it sits on active fault lines that can sometimes rupture with unpredictable power and violence.

ARTHUR'S PASS NATIONAL PARK

One of the first places protected in Canterbury for its obvious scenery and surviving natural character was the wild headwaters of the Waimakariri River, about midway along the most direct route west from Christchurch across the Southern Alps. Largely as the result of a long campaign for protection by pioneer botanist Dr Leonard Cockayne, and a large numbers of Canterbury residents who had begun visiting the area since the West Coast railway had reached Arthur's Pass, this mountainous area became the South Island's first national park in 1929. It is still the most accessible national park to a large population centre in New Zealand and is popular with trampers, mountaineers and hunters as well as day excursionists.

Today it remains the quintessential South Island trans-alpine national park with its swift and dramatic transition from the dry eastern side of the Southern Alps to the very much wetter west. In terms of Canterbury high-country landscapes, it also provides excellent roadside examples of the kind of landforms and scenery that dominate the whole of the eastern side of the Southern Alps between the Lewis Pass and Aoraki/Mt Cook – the wide, open, braided river beds; tawny tussock grasslands; dry, open forests of mountain beech; and rapidly eroding greywacke mountains whose scree-covered flanks bear witness to the fact that the process that created the Canterbury Plains is still recycling shattered mountains down to lower altitudes.

AORAKI/MOUNT COOK NATIONAL PARK

Aoraki/Mount Cook National Park (70,699 hectares) contains all but a few of New Zealand's highest mountains. At its heart rears Aoraki/Mt Cook (3,754 metres), New Zealand's highest peak, first climbed in 1894 by three intrepid New Zealanders – Tom Fyfe, George Graham and Jack Clarke.

While reserves were set aside as early as the 1880s in this premier alpine region, for many years the 'Aoraki Domain' and the 'Tasman Reserve' were leased out to private interests (the Mt Cook Motor Company who owned the Hermitage had the Aoraki Domain). This led to friction when the Hermitage started trying to charge the general public for access to walk and climb in the reserve. Arthur P Harper, a stalwart of the New Zealand Alpine Club, was instrumental in forming the Federated Mountain Clubs (FMC), a national collection of climbing and tramping clubs who pressured the government not to renew this lease and instead turn the area into a national park. Mount Cook National Park was gazetted in 1953 and in recognition of Ngai Tahu's (the South Island's largest iwi) special relationship with the mountain the park was renamed Aoraki/Mount Cook National Park in 1998.

FOLLOWING PAGE Aoraki/Mt Cook from Mueller Hut, Aoraki/Mount Cook National Park

Evening light on Aoraki/Mt Cook from the Sealy Range, Aoraki/Mount Cook National Park

Mt Cook buttercups, Hooker Valley, Aoraki/Mount Cook National Park
FOLLOWING PAGE Larch trees in autumn and the Mt Cook massif, Lake Pukaki

Southeasterly cloud spilling over the Main Divide, Mt Sefton (left) and Aoraki/Mt Cook in the distance, Aoraki/Mount Cook National Park

Terminal lake of the Mueller Glacier and Mt Sefton, Aoraki/Mount Cook National Park

Lake Tekapo and the Southern Alps from Mt John, Mackenzie Country, Canterbury

Lake Heron and the Taylor Range, Ashburton Lakes High Country

Mountain beech forest, Edwards Valley, Arthur's Pass National Park

Cameron River and the Arrowsmith Range, Ashburton Lakes High Country

Opihi River near Temuka

Lyttelton Harbour, Banks Peninsula

Seaward Kaikoura Range from the Kaikoura Peninsula

Nelson and Marlborough

The top of New Zealand's South Island contains a greater diversity of landforms and scenery than any other region, and also occupies the country's main biological cross-roads – the meeting place of warmer north and cooler south, wetter west and drier east. As a consequence, some 45 per cent of its total area is today under some form of permanent protection, including three national parks (Abel Tasman, Nelson Lakes and Kahurangi), two large conservation parks (in the Richmond and Kaikoura ranges) and the huge (180,000 hectare) Molesworth Recreation Reserve.

This general landscape diversity is most clearly demonstrated by the region's magnificent range of coastal landscapes. These include the dramatic Kaikoura coast with its rich seabird and marine mammal fauna; the labyrinth of waterways in the Marlborough Sounds; the north-facing Tasman and Golden bays, with their numerous safe, sandy beaches and barrier-enclosed tidal inlets; the far-famed beauty of Abel Tasman National Park; the 30-kilometre sand finger and wetland of international importance at Farewell Spit; and the dramatic sea-cliffs, coves and beaches at the northern end of the South Island's wild West Coast. Increasingly the region to the west of Nelson is being recognised as one of New Zealand's biological hot spots and a key area for plant and animal endemism; that is containing species found nowhere else on earth. Many of these species are now protected within New Zealand's second largest national park.

KAHURANGI NATIONAL PARK

No other national park in New Zealand matches the diversity of rocks, landforms and indigenous flora found in Kahurangi. Within a basic pattern of five distinct assemblages of parent rocks running through the park from north to south are New Zealand's most ancient sedimentary and volcanic rocks as well as the country's oldest fossils. This extraordinary range of landforms,

Queen Charlotte Sound from Mt Stokes, Marlborough Sounds

born of a complex geology, includes a number of extensive high tablelands or plateaux, the northernmost glaciated cirques and valleys in the South Island, and, in the eastern marble belt, some of the deepest, longest and oldest cave systems in the Southern Hemisphere.

A similar diversity occurs in the park's biota. More than half of New Zealand's 2,500 species of native higher plants are found within the park – including 80 per cent of the country's alpine plant species. On the wildlife front, along with the important habitat it provides for many threatened species (including blue duck, rock wren, New Zealand falcon and kea), Kahurangi National Park is the main stronghold for great spotted kiwi (which are confined to the ranges in the northwest of the South Island) and also the main centre of evolution and speciation for *Powelliphanta* land snails.

The other outstanding attraction of this park is its magnificent network of tramping tracks and huts, including the Heaphy Track that takes in the full sweep of the park's diversity.

ABEL TASMAN NATIONAL PARK

New Zealand's smallest national park is also one of its prettiest and most visited. The park was created on the 300th anniversary of the first European sighting of New Zealand by Dutch sea-captain Abel Tasman in 1642, following two decades of lobbying by Nelsonian Perrine Moncrieff. The daughter of a wealthy English family, Moncrieff had moved to Nelson in the early 1920s and would dedicate the rest of her life to the protection of New Zealand native birds and forests. In all, she was responsible for the protection of more than 50,000 hectares in the Nelson region, a truly heroic contribution towards preserving the region's priceless natural heritage.

The outstanding feature of the park is without doubt its beautiful coastline of golden beaches, sandy tidal inlets and bold granite headlands, which each year bring upwards of 150,000 walkers to its coastal track, while thousands of others kayak the adjoining coastal waters. Elsewhere, however, the park has a number of other highly distinctive landforms, including outcrops of granite tors and core-stones scattered along its much less frequented Inland Track, and the massive 176 metre chasm of Harwood's Hole (New Zealand's deepest

Sawcut Gorge, Limestone Hill Scenic Reserve, Marlborough

vertical shaft) in the eerie marble landscape at Canaan near the park's southwestern boundary.

NELSON LAKES NATIONAL PARK

Nelson Lakes seems to be one of those places that became a national park with comparatively little fuss, perhaps because there was little interest in forestry, farming or hydro electricity generation in the mountain valleys at this northern end of the Southern Alps. Established in 1956 to protect the large lakes Rotoiti and Rotoroa and their mountain catchments, the park was enlarged in 1983 by the addition of a further 43,000 hectares in the Matakitaki and Glenroy valleys south of Murchison. Besides the two large lakes, key features of the park include its beautiful, long, beech-forested valleys and its extensive network of tramping tracks and huts.

In the absence of a major tourist attraction, the park has been valued for more than 50 years for its peace, tranquillity and low key 'family' atmosphere. Lakes Rotoiti and Rotoroa are both easily accessible from state highways (especially Lake Rotoiti) and have camping areas, easy walking tracks and boat launching facilities. A notable recent addition to the attractions of a visit to Lake Rotoiti is its intensively managed 'mainland island' wildlife sanctuary. This is one of the best and most easily accessible places in which to experience the results of the Department of Conservation's efforts to replicate in mainland New Zealand the sanctuary conditions of predator-free offshore islands.

Lakes Rotoiti and Rotoroa are also the headwaters of the Buller River; a major landscape feature carving a route from here to the West Coast. The Buller is one of the largest undammed rivers in the country and as a consequence the lakes are an important breeding ground for eels. There are some monster eels in the lake with records of some weighing more than 20 kilograms. Eels can live in the lake for up to 50 years before reaching maturity and then making the long final journey to the sea to breed.

MARLBOROUGH SOUNDS

In the northeast, the Marlborough Sounds are New Zealand's most intricate labyrinth of coastal waterways, and a classic example of a landscape resulting from 'drowned valleys'.

This distinctive area was created by subsidence of this part of the earth's crust as the Pacific Plate subducted below the Australian Plate to the west. As sea levels rose up to 60 meters at the end of the last ice age, sea water flooded into the region's former river valleys leaving the ridges as steep-sided tentacles of land reaching out towards the distant ocean.

Although large areas of the Sounds have in the past been modified for farming and forestry there remains a strong ambience of natural character about the region as a whole, partly from its more than 50 scenic and nature reserves, and partly through the now widespread reversion to native vegetation in places which have proved uneconomic for farming and forestry. A number of islands within the Sounds play a critical role in threatened species conservation, providing (among much else) the country's most important sanctuaries for tuatara, unique Maud Island and Hamilton's frogs, two rare geckos, South Island saddlebacks, king shags and juvenile Okarito brown kiwi. Elsewhere in the Sounds, holiday homes dot much of the long shoreline and the sheltered waterways are the most popular location in the South Island for boating and recreational fishing.

KAIKOURA RANGES AND MOLESWORTH PLATEAU

The southern parts of the Marlborough landscape are defined by four key components, each of which is distinctive in a national context. The most prominent feature of the region is the Inland and Seaward Kaikoura ranges, the former containing the highest mountains in New Zealand north of the Mount Cook region. Dividing these ranges is the long, twisting course of the Clarence River which for the most part flows through some of the country's most arid and treeless mountain terrain. In its upper reaches the Clarence flows in a great arc south of the high inland Molesworth plateau through landscapes that often seem to belong more to Tibet than they do to New Zealand. In contrast, along the coastal flanks of the Seaward Kaikoura Range native forest is still comparatively widespread, providing one of the few places along the 950 kilometres of State Highway 1 between Picton and Bluff where native vegetation remains a significant component of an eastern South Island landscape.

FOLLOWING PAGE Evening light on the Boulder Bank, Nelson

Appletree Bay, Abel Tasman National Park

Coastline near Totaranui estuary, Abel Tasman National Park

Archway Islands, Wharariki Beach, Golden Bay

Archway Islands, Wharariki Beach, Golden Bay

Karst near the summit of Mt Owen, Mt Patriarch in the distance, Kahurangi National Park
OPPOSITE PAGE Spring snowfall, the Tablelands, Kahurangi National Park

Spaniard, Lake Angelus, Nelson Lakes National Park

Lake Angelus, Nelson Lakes National Park

Hinapouri Tarn and Mt Angelus, Nelson Lakes National Park

West Sabine River, Nelson Lakes National Park

Western North Island

Exposed to the full force of the prevailing weather, the western coastline of the North Island is an uncompromising landscape comprising rugged coastal cliffs, iron sand beaches and rocky headlines. Three large tidal inlets at Kawhia, Raglan and Aotea open to the Tasman Sea, all of which are important estuarine ecosystems. The coastline near Raglan Harbour is also famous for having one of the country's most reliable surfing breaks.

Inland from the coast is some of the finest farming country in New Zealand, particularly in the fertile soils and verdant grass of the Waikato Basin. Little native forest remains in lowland Waikato but in the hills of the Kaimai–Mamaku ranges, Mt Pirongia and Maungatautiri, native forests provide a refuge for endemic plants and animals. Other natural areas of the Waikato include the internationally significant wetlands at Whangamarino and Kopuatai, remnants of once common natural ecosystems that have mostly been drained for agriculture.

The waters of the mighty Waikato River start on the slopes of the Central North Island mountains where they flow into the Tongaririo River and Lake Taupo. As the Waikato proper begins at Lake Taupo, it continues to gather up water from this huge catchment to become the longest river in New Zealand. Through a series of eight dams and nine power stations, the power of the Waikato is harnessed for hydro electricity as it meanders its way towards the sea at Port Waikato.

South of the Waikato basin the contours of the land become progressively more broken. While the Waikato is more known for dairy farming, the hill country of the King Country better suits sheep and beef farming. However both landscapes were settled under an historical cloud.

The regional name King Country dates from the time when the Maori King Movement

Sunset on Mt Taranaki, Egmont National Park

took refuge here from the colonial forces that invaded the Waikato in the 1860s. The conflict arose over the tribes of the area refusing to sell the incredibly valuable land of the Waikato to the colonial government. The invasion of the Waikato was perhaps the lowest point in what historians now call the New Zealand Wars. The action saw some Maori loyal to the Crown line up with colonial troops against the authority of the King Movement in a conflict that was a fundamental breach of the Treaty of Waitangi. Through a number of settlements, including one regarding the river itself, the Crown has compensated Tainui, a confederation of the four main Waikato tribes, for this troubled period in New Zealand history.

On the junction of these two regions is a band of limestone containing typical karst country features of caves, sinkholes and outcrops. The centrepiece of this geology is the glowworm caves at Waitomo that have been a tourist attraction since the early 1900s.

Further south, the almost perfectly symmetrical volcanic cone of Mt Taranaki dominates the view across the North Taranaki Bight. On a geological timescale, Taranaki is a relatively new landscape created by thousands of years of andesitic eruptions. The huge ringplain around the mountain is today fertile rural grasslands, mostly used for diary farming, which, along with gas and oil, is the backbone of the Taranaki economy.

EGMONT NATIONAL PARK

Mt Taranaki sits at the centre of Egmont National Park, New Zealand's second national park gazetted in 1900.

While the mountain and remaining forests are without doubt worthy of national park status, the park has a chequered history. The core reserves were set aside for a national park in 1881 from lands confiscated as a result of the 1860s Taranaki land wars. There have been various attempts to right this wrong over the years, including the 1978 Egmont Vesting Act where the park was briefly handed back to a local Maori trust board before being gifted back to the nation.

The park's landscape continues to be shaped by the high rainfall that frequents the Taranaki region. The mountain itself seems to generate its own climate when moisture-laden winds

Kapiti Island from the coastline near Pukerua Bay, Wellington from the Tasman Sea rapidly cool after rising up the mountain slopes. This frequently results in the mountain revealing itself in the morning and evening light, while being cloaked in cloud for most of the day.

In the northwestern part of the park lies the Pouakai Range, the eroded remnants of an extinct volcano of once similar size and shape to Mt Taranaki. Mt Taranaki itself was born some 120,000 years ago just as the older vent around Pouakai died out. The Pouakai vent has been gradually whittled down by the weather while Taranaki continued to grow in height. Taranaki was last active in 1776 and volcanologists currently consider the mountain dormant. Trapped between these two volcanic forms is the Ahukawakawa Swamp: an impressive sphagnum wetland area containing a number of unique ecosystems and surrounded by forest distinguished by its prevalent mountain cedar trees.

WHANGANUI NATIONAL PARK

Although the Whanganui River itself is not part of the national park, it is the main way for people to access and enjoy the park today. Long before the park was created, the river played an important role as part of the transport route between Wellington and Auckland. Travellers caught the train from Wellington to the Whanganui River and then boarded one of the steam-driven paddleboats that transported them to Pipiriki. From Pipiriki they embarked on smaller boats that continued all the way to Taumarunui; a river journey of some 234 kilometres. From here the train continued to Auckland.

These riverboats were the brainchild of Alexander Hatrick who in the 1890s commissioned the first steam driven boat. At the height of the riverboat era 12 boats operated on the Whanganui, which was promoted in tourism publications as the 'Rhine of Maoriland'. Hatrick, spurred on by the success of his business, also convinced the government to protect the land on either side of the river as a scenic reserve. These reserves later formed the core of the national park.

By 1908 the North Island's main trunk railway line was complete and this signalled a slow decline in the Whanganui's popularity as a tourist destination. The creation of the park in 1986 reignited interest in travelling the river. Like early Maori, modern day visitors usually travel by canoe and kayak.

Local Maori have a long relationship with the river and they too utilised the river as a practical North Island transport link. Many marae remain places of activity along the river and at Maraekowhai are historic niu (ceremonial peace poles) erected by followers of the Pai Marire movement (a syncretic Maori religion mixing biblical themes with traditional beliefs) in 1864.

As the riverboat era came to an end, the government began to settle serviceman returning from the First World War in the Whanganui hinterland. These 'soldier-farmers' had a tough time breaking in the gorge-riven forested landscape and the farms were not a success. Most of this land has now been incorporated into Whanganui National Park. Some of the historical sites from this period, such as the Bridge to Nowhere, are among the most visited parts of the park.

KAPITI COAST & WELLINGTON

South of Whanganui the western coast opens up in a long sandy arc that stretches down to the rugged greywacke coast near Kapiti. Kapiti Island, located offshore from Paraparaumu, is one of New Zealand's earliest nature reserves, set aside in 1897. This predator-free island is an important refuge for North Island kaka, saddlebacks and takahe as well as little spotted kiwi and stitchbirds. Many of these species are now either rare or absent from mainland New Zealand, although saddlebacks, stitchbirds and kiwi have recently been reintroduced to Wellington's Zealandia sanctuary.

Wellington, another New Zealand Company settlement started in 1839, became the capital of New Zealand after the Parliament was moved to this central location from Auckland in 1865. Sitting at the southern end of an extensive harbour, Wellington is a compact city, contained within hills that have prevented the sprawl more common in other cities. This advantage, combined with its vibrant arts and culture scene, make Wellington an attractive place to live and more than compensate for the regular buffeting it receives from the westerly weather.

Cape Egmont Lighthouse, Taranaki

The Bridge to Nowhere, Whanganui National Park
FOLLOWING PAGE Mt Taranaki from the Pouakai Range, Egmont National Park

Mt Taranaki from the Pouakai Range, Egmont National Park
OPPOSITE PAGE Bells Falls, Egmont National Park

Waireinga/Bridal Veil Falls, Waikato

Mt Taranaki from Whitecliffs, Tongaporutu

East Coast and Wairarapa

The eastern side of the North Island has climate characteristics similar to the eastern South Island. The North Island axial mountain range is a significant hurdle for the prevailing westerly weather and, as a consequence of this orographic lift, the air on the East Coast is much hotter and drier than most other parts of New Zealand.

The East Coast retains its special Maori heritage with many people of the iwi Ngati Porou resisting the drift to urban centres and retaining their strong bond to their homelands. Traditional marae and meeting houses play an important part in this bond and are dotted throughout the East Coast landscape.

Sheep farming and forestry are the two mainstays of the East Coast economy. In the days before roads and trucking transport, much of the wool was shipped direct from the nearest practical shoreline. At Tolaga Bay a large historic jetty extends out into the sea as a reminder of the days when shipping was the main connection to these remote rural communities.

The East Coast also has an important historical connection with James Cook's first voyage around the world on the HMS *Endeavour*. In October 1769 he anchored in what is now known as Cook's Cove near Tolaga Bay. This was the first significant landfall on his circumnavigation of New Zealand and the crew spent some time here interacting peacefully with the local Maori population. A walkway from Tolaga Bay leads out to the site and the landscape features here are still identifiable from the descriptions in journals of the voyage. Numerous other coastal features also retain the names that Cook gave them including Young Nick's Head near Gisborne; first sighted by 12 year-old Nicholas Young (the servant to the ship's surgeon) and the first sighting of New Zealand by Cook's crew.

Further south, Hawke's Bay is a fertile region

for horticulture and viticulture and the two main towns in the region have distinct architectural styles. In February 1931 the towns of Napier and Hastings were completely devastated by an earthquake. The government moved quickly to rebuild the towns and embraced the austere Art Deco style of the times. In the case of Napier, today it is celebrated as one of the most complete and interesting collections of Art Deco buildings in the world. Hastings also adopted the Art Deco style but added in some interesting Spanish Mission style buildings that give the city a distinctly different architectural flavour to Napier.

The landscape of much of the Wairarapa differs little from the Hawke's Bay with similar climatic conditions in the lee of the axial mountains with sheep and grape country being the main feature of the rural landscape.

TE UREWERA NATIONAL PARK

Te Urewera National Park (214,000 hectares) is the largest expanse of native forest left in the North Island and forever will be associated with the local Tuhoe people. Perhaps no other tribe has so consistently asserted its independence and/or been subjected to as many historical injustices as Tuhoe. The government severely sanctioned Tuhoe after they harboured the Maori prophet and rebel Te Kooti Rikirangi in the 1860s, and again in the early 1900s imprisoned the peaceful leader Rua Kenana who had sought to establish an independent community in Te Urewera. To an extent the sombre beauty of Te Urewera reflects these dark periods of the area's history.

The most visited part of the park is the twin lakes of Waikaremoana and Waikareiti. Of the two, Lake Waikaremoana is a geologically recent feature having been formed some 2,200 years ago when an earthquake released a rockslide off the Ngamoko Range damming the Aniwaniwa Stream. Waikareiti is older, having been created by a similar process some 12,000 years ago.

The Ureweras also contain one of the largest remaining populations of North Island kokako, a rare native New Zealand bird with an unmistakable and hauntingly beautiful call. In the Northern Ureweras a large forest restoration project traps predators over a number of key areas covering some 9,000 hectares. North Island kiwi and blue duck are amongst the other rare bird species protected by this programme.

THE FOREST PARKS

The eastern North Island is the 'land of Forest Parks' with six of the island's 13 forest parks located in this zone – Raukumara, Aorangi, Kaweka, Ruahine, Tararua and Rimutaka. Aorangi is the smallest of these and the only one not on the main axial mountain range.

The Raukumara Ranges in the north are perhaps the most rugged, and remain largely untracked. Only a handful of huts exist in the area, and the range contains the North Island's largest wilderness area. Snaking sinuously through the western edge of the 39,650 hectare Raukumara Wilderness Area is the Motu River, one of New Zealand's wildest rivers which provides a fine multi-day rafting trip. The highest point on the range, Mt Hikurangi (1,752 meters), is the first place on mainland New Zealand to see the sunrise and the highest non-volcanic peak in the North Island.

Formed in 1974, Kaweka Forest Park (59,300 hectares) is a popular hunting and tramping place for Hawke's Bay locals. While the eastern parts of the range are heavily eroded by past misuse through over-grazing and fires, the western valleys retain their original forest cover. Beech forest dominates the Kawekas, but large areas of open tops exist too, and peaks like North Kaweka (1,707 metres) and Kaweka J (1,724 metres) are among the highest of the main axial mountain range.

Perhaps one of the most underrated parts of our protected wild places is the Ruahine Ranges, yet they contain some of the more interesting landscapes in the North Island. It is also one of the North Island's key enclaves of biodiversity, particularly around the northern Ruahines near the Mangaohane Plateau. Here the ancient mountain cedar forests reach their highest expression, and in the forests near this area North Island Brown kiwi, native falcons, blue duck, long-tailed bats and even a species of native land snail all find refuge. Limestone makes an unexpected appearance in this northwestern part of the Ruahine Forest Park too, with resulting influences in both the topography and ecology.

For more than a century, the Tararua Ranges have been a popular place for Wellingtonians to escape for weekend tramping and hunting trips. Many of New Zealand's earliest tramping clubs formed in the surrounding cities and towns, and most of these clubs played a large role developing tracks and huts in the area, as well as exploring and mapping it, from the 1920s onwards. These clubs forged a strong identity around the range, resulting in two proposals for the area to become a national park in the 1930s and again in the early 1950s. The New Zealand Forest Service, who managed the area, wanted to maintain control, and came up with a compromise by creating a new style of park in 1954, when the Tararuas became New Zealand's first forest park.

For the next 33 years the park was managed under a 'multiple use' policy and this wide mandate enabled the Forest Service to manage parts of the ranges for everything from exotic forestry to areas set aside for water and soil conservation. They also greatly expanded the number of huts and tracks in the park and this network is now a recognised part of the quintessential New Zealand back-country experience.

The Tararua Ranges differ subtly from their northern counterparts in the Ruahines by being slightly lower and with sharper, more rugged tops. The mountains here are also subjected to some of the most extreme weather in New Zealand as the prevailing westerly winds funnel through Cook Strait. On average the tops are covered in cloud for more than 250 days of every year and subjected to over 5,000 millimetres of annual rainfall on their westerly slopes.

South of the Tararua Range, where State Highway 2 cuts a winding path over the ridge crest, the axial mountains become the Rimutaka Range, which is also another forest park. These forested ranges end at Turakirae Head, on the edge of Cook Strait, where the main fault-line dips under the sea. Rimutaka Forest Park's largest river, the Orongorongo, is an enormously popular haunt of trampers, who enjoy overnight family bush trips in the valley's many private and public huts.

Castlepoint Lighthouse, Wairarapa

Silver beech forest, Cone Ridge, Tararua Forest Park

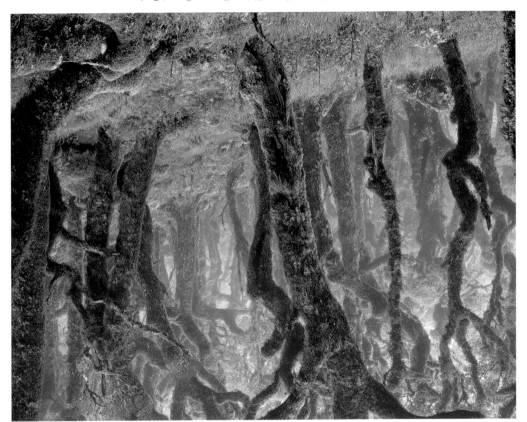

Korokoro Falls, Te Urewera National Park

Sunrise on Kaiaua Beach north of Gisborne, East Coast
OPPOSITE Te Mata Peak, Hawke's Bay

Te Atua Mahuru, Colenso Spur, Ruahine Forest Park

Tussock grasslands near Ruahine Corner, Ruahine Forest Park

East Island and East Cape

The Central North Island

Running through the centre of the North Island, from Mt Ruapehu to White Island in the Bay of Plenty, is a line of geothermal activity and volcanism that highlights New Zealand's position on the 'Pacific Ring of Fire'. Boiling mud, geysers, steam vents, strange geothermal pools and impressive volcanic mountains all make this region an exceptional place for seeing the Earth in this primordial form.

The Taupo–Rotorua highway follows this main line of geothermal activity providing access to six main sites worthy of a visit. Whakarewarewa and Hell's Gate in Rotorua are followed further south by Waimangu, Wai-o-tapu and Orakei Korako; all with their own specific attractions. At Taupo, the Craters of the Moon are a spectacular finish to this geothermal highway, where boardwalks lead around active steam vents and boiling mud.

Lake Taupo sits in the centre of the North Island and in geological terms is a caldera of the largest volcanic eruption known to have occurred on the Earth in the past 70,000 years. Around 27,000 years ago, in what is known as the Oruanui Eruption, a massive explosion blasted this crater in the Earth's surface that today is filled by Lake Taupo.

Taupo's last big eruption is thought to have occurred in AD 186. Scientists have pinpointed this date from both the geological estimate and historic Chinese and Roman texts that record a change in the Earth's atmosphere for this period. Much of the central North Island is covered with a layer of ash and pumice from the eruption, and deposits have even been found on Pacific Islands far from New Zealand. Standing on the seemingly benign shores of the lake, it is easy to be somewhat oblivious to Taupo's violent geological past. On most days Taupo seems a place of peaceful calm where the waters of New Zealand's largest lake lap gently on the shores.

Many more eruptions along the Taupo Volcanic Zone have occurred since the human occupation

North Crater of Mt Tongaririo with Mt Ngauruhoe and Ruapehu in the distance, Tongariro National Park

of New Zealand. The most destructive was the Tarawera eruption of 1886, which destroyed the famous Pink and White Terraces – perhaps the most beautiful geothermal formations the world has ever known. At least 153 people died in this event, almost all of whom were residents of the Maori villages near the mountain.

Mt Ngauruhoe has had periodic outbursts, lastly in 1972, and more recently, Mt Ruapehu erupted spectacularly in the mid 1990s. Ruapehu gave plenty of warning with increased seismic activity, and when the eruption started in September 1995 there were no casualties. Mt Ruapehu's Crater Lake has refilled since a second eruption in 1996, but the mountain continues to show signs of activity from time to time.

TONGARIRO NATIONAL PARK

The scenic beauty of this high volcanic plateau, with its three prominent volcanoes, was recognised quite early in the nation's history. The story of its protection as New Zealand's first national park perhaps started with Sir William Fox who was Premier of New Zealand several times between 1856 and 1873. Fox had travelled to the United States and visited the world's first national park in the thermal wonderland of Yellowstone. As Premier, Fox supported Maori land rights and it is likely that this, along with seeing other thermal scenic wonders of the North Island privatised, prompted him to be an early promoter of the parks idea. There was a degree of pragmatism in Fox's support for parks as a practical response to a complex array of political issues. Maori land loss, changes to the Native Land Act (which attempted to individualise Maori land holding) and increasing conservation issues with the conversion of land for agriculture, all contributed to the genesis of the park idea in New Zealand.

It was left to the mountain's owners to make the initial gift of land to form New Zealand's first national park. On the 23rd of September 1887 Horonuku Te HeuHeu of Ngati Tuwharetoa signed the deed of gift that bestowed custodianship of the highest summits of the three main volcanoes to the New Zealand public. This initial area was 2,630 hectares but over time the government purchased more land surrounding this until six years later the Tongariro National Park Bill was passed,

Sunrise on Mt Ngauruhoe, Tongariro National Park

protecting some 25,000 hectares. Over time more land has been added and today Tongariro National Park covers some 80,000 hectares and is recognised as a UNESCO World Heritage Area: one of the few places acknowledged for both its natural and cultural importance.

In summer the park is popular with walkers, while in winter the park turns into something of a winter playground with Whakapapa and Turoa the two largest skifields in the North Island.

WHIRINAKI & PUREORA FOREST PARKS

Today, we walk through the tall, primeval podocarp forests of Whirinaki and Pureora and it seems hard to believe that only 30 years ago there was a bitter conservation fight to save these trees from the sawmill. What to current generations seems obvious beauty was part of a government industry that had been steadily logging these forests since the late 1920s.

The Forest Service ran the mills in question; this former government department occupies a mixed place in our conservation and recreation history. On one hand it was responsible for ensuring that many forested catchments were protected from the bush-burn practices of the late nineteenth century, and actively engaged in the battle against those who would have converted all of New Zealand to farmland. However, on the other hand the Forest Service also had a mandate to provide the country with timber, and so sought to exploit some lowland forests in the central North Island not considered as important for catchment protection.

Aggressive logging areas of lowland forest, based often on arguments that the trees had 'reached maturity', and so called forest 'enrichment' schemes of inter-planting native forest with what are now considered 'weed' trees, all contributed to a general decline in forest health. By the early 1970s it was quite obvious that public attitudes to logging had changed and that habitat loss of our remaining lowland forests was having a detrimental effect on native bird populations.

Protests came to a head in the mid-1970s at Pureora, where the Forest Service began logging old growth podocarp forest that was prime habitat for the endangered North Island kokako. The Wildlife Service had recommended this area for protection, but it took the actions of determined tree-sitters to get the Forest Service to back down. Finally, in 1978, the Forest Service bowed to public pressure, ended native forest logging there, and formed Pureora Forest Park.

But disputes over logging continued at Whirinaki into the 1980s, and it was not until 1984 that the Forest Service largely abandoned its mill at the nearby town of Minginui.

In 1987 the Labour Government amalgamated the Forest Service, Lands & Survey and the Wildlife Service into the Department of Conservation, a far-sighted decision that enabled one government department to manage protected areas with clearer conservation goals.

KAIMANAWA FOREST PARK

On the eastern side of the Desert Road is Kaimanawa Forest Park which, along with the Kaweka Ranges further east, encompasses the widest expanse of the North Island mountain axis. Geologically, the mountain ranges are comprised largely of greywacke rock thrust up out of the Earth's crust in the last few million years by continental collision.

The geology of the western Kaimanawas shows the influence of Tongariro volcanism and in places attractive waterways flow through ancient lava flows of andesite and ignimbrite rock. The Pillars of Hercules and Tree Trunk Gorge are two accessible places where the Tongariro River narrows before flowing through a spectacular volcanic chasm.

The 78,000 hectare Kaimanawa Forest Park was formed in 1969 and contains the headwaters of the Mohaka, Rangitikei and Ngaruroro Rivers – all important for fishing, tramping and rafting. Both the Mohaka and Ngaruroro flow out to Hawke's Bay through Kaweka Forest Park.

From a recreational point of view, the Kaimanawas are best known for hunting, particularly because they contain the largest herd of Sika deer in New Zealand. Trampers find plenty of interesting trips in the area too, and a traverse through to the eastern Kawekas takes about a week.

FOLLOWING PAGE Farmland near the western side of Mt Ruapehu

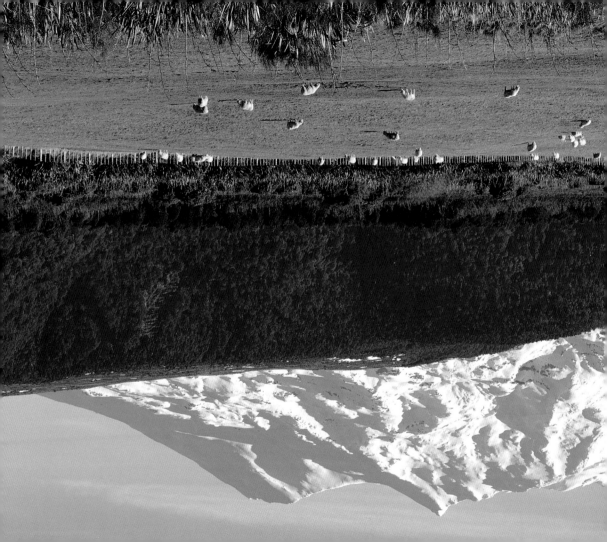

Blue Lake and Mt Ngauruhoe, Tongaririo National Park

Tree Trunk Gorge, Kaimanawa Forest Park

The geothermal Champagne Pool, Wai-o-Tapu Scenic Reserve, Rotorua

Pohutu Geyser, Whakarewarewa Thermal Area, Rotorua

Waipunga Falls, Waipunga River near Taupo

Te Whaiti-Nui-a-Toi Canyon, Whirinaki Forest Park

Coromandel and the North

THE FAR NORTH, HOKIANGA & BAY OF ISLANDS

Even the clouds feel different in the far north. With its semi-tropical climate and sandy beaches it seems more like a separate Pacific Island, shunning its material connection to the temperate mainland of New Zealand. Indeed, the landscapes around Cape Reinga were not so long ago islands, which have been connected to the mainland by drifting sand – a geographical feature known as a tombolo.

For Maori, Cape Reinga itself holds much spiritual importance and is known by another name of Te Rerenga Wairua meaning the 'leaping-off place of the spirits'. Off the tip of the cape the wild Tasman Sea collides with the seemingly endless Pacific and this meeting of two great oceans off the coast seems to underline the spiritual feel of this landscape.

Visible to the west and south of Cape Reinga are the magnificent sand dunes at Te Paki. These are the most extensive dune lands in New Zealand and lie at the northern end of New Zealand's longest beach – Ninety Mile Beach.

At the base of the far north peninsula, the town of Kaitaia feels like a door to more familiar rural North Island landscapes. Fertile farmland and plentiful small bays mix with patches of remnant forest and broken hill country. Many quaint country wooden churches, of all denominations but mainly Anglican, Wesleyan and Catholic, pepper the Northland landscape: a living reminder of the fierce competition for souls that took place here in the 1800s.

Probably the three main reasons that Europeans first settled in the Bay of Islands were the mild climate, attractive timber of the kauri forests and the large Maori population with whom to trade. It is little wonder then that the Bay of Islands became the 'cradle of New Zealand' in reference to its birthplace as the most far-flung part of the British Empire. The

Lone pohutukawa tree above Coromandel Harbour

signing of the Treaty at Waitangi on the 6th of February 1840 between Maori chiefs and the British Crown's representatives marked the start of modern New Zealand; the first tentative steps to a Westminster style democracy and an agreement between two world views that is still being discussed.

In the context of the times, with the British empire already in decline, the Treaty was an attempt at empire expansion in a civilised way. In the time of Queen Victoria the British empire had came to see itself as a force of progressive good in the world, and the Treaty can be viewed as part of this 'empire of good intentions'. The Treaty of Waitangi still continues to cast both shadow and light over modern New Zealand. In essence, the shadow still remains in part because the Crown (meaning New Zealand government) historically has not always fulfilled its responsibilities, while the light is that it is still a document with meaning that creates discussion, debate and sharing in New Zealand's own evolving democracy. Knowing all this makes the trip to Waitangi a moving one for many New Zealanders.

On the western coast lies the Hokianga Harbour. The full Maori name for the harbour is 'Te Hokianga-nui-a-Kupe' – 'the place of Kupe's great return' – in reference to the legendary Polynesian explorer who according to oral history settled in the Hokianga in 925 AD.

By the time European settlers arrived, the Hokianga must have seemed one of the richest places in New Zealand with its harbour, surrounded by majestic kauri forest, sustaining many Maori tribes and villages. A fledgling boat building industry was started by European settlers in the 1820s and by the 1850s as many as 20 ships were anchored in the harbour loading kauri stripped from the hillsides. With the forests largely gone, the Hokianga fell on hard times but more recently Te Kohanga o Te Tai Tokerau – 'the nest of the northern people' – is beginning to trade on the magnetic appeal the locals will say it never really lost.

THE KAURI FORESTS

The sheer size and grandness of large kauri trees means that walking through a grove of them can astonish visitors in much the same way as witnessing a landscape like Milford Sound or Mt Cook for the first time. Kauri take

Coastal pohutukawa trees, Coromandel Peninsula

a long time to mature and some of the greatest remaining trees are more than 1,000 years old. Scientists estimate the largest known remaining kauri, Tane Mahuta, is between 1,250 and 2,500 years old.

Tane Mahuta lies in the Waipoua Forest Sanctuary that now protects much of the last of the great Northland kauri forests. More than 98 per cent of these forests were cut down for timber, most of which ended up in virtually every timber house built in New Zealand before 1940. In this short sighted 'rush to destruction', many great trees were cut down while others were lost to uncontrolled burning. What may have been the oldest and largest kauri tree was lost to fire in the 1880s near Dargaville. Kairaru was thought to be 4,000 years old and twice the size of Tane Mahuta.

The State Forest Service continued cutting down kauri near Waipoua until the late 1940s and agreed to establish a forest sanctuary in 1952 only after a national outcry and ongoing public protest. Today, kauri trees are threatened by the new risk of disease. A new *Phytophthora* genus was discovered in New Zealand in the 1970s and has since spread to the Northland kauri forests. This disease, known as kauri collar rot, has the potential to devastate the remaining kauri forests.

AUCKLAND AND THE WAITAKERE RANGES

Straddling the isthmus between two great harbours – the Waitemata and the Manukau – New Zealand's largest city is without doubt one of the most beautiful cities in the southern hemisphere. Auckland is built entirely on a volcanic zone and the nearly 50 extinct volcanic cones, vents and ancient calderas are the landscapes that lend Auckland much of its distinctive topography. Many of these features were formed only 10–50,000 years ago and some of the more notable volcanic scoria cones like Mt Eden, Mt Wellington, One Tree Hill and North Head are prominent parts of the city skyline. The most recently active volcano in the Auckland zone is also an inescapable part of most Auckland panoramas. Rangitoto Island last erupted 600 years ago and today its lava flows are covered with pohutukawa forest and the island is a popular day trip from Auckland.

Rangitoto is one of many islands in the

Hauraki Gulf, Auckland's major marine recreation area that on many days is filled with boats of all shapes and sizes. This temperate archipelago is protected by the Hauraki Gulf Marine Park, essentially a national park of the sea, covering most islands in the gulf including Great Barrier Island, Tiritiri Matangi Island, Kawau Island and extending all the way across to parts of the Coromandel coastline.

The other highly valued part of the Auckland landscape is the wild western beaches that border the coastal forest of the Waitakere Ranges. Karekare, Piha and further north, Murawai and Bethells Beach, are all coastal places used by Aucklanders as an escape from the urban world. Most of the Waitakere Ranges were logged for kauri to build Auckland but the regenerating coastal forest is today laced with popular walking tracks.

COROMANDEL

The Coromandel Ranges, while only reaching a maximum height of 892 metres, dominate the peninsula landscape. The spine of the ranges comprises eroded and rugged remnants of volcanic peaks that were active over two million years ago. This volcanic activity is long extinct but geothermal hot springs are still active on the peninsula and those at Hot Water Beach provide the novelty of a hot bath on a sandy beach.

Coromandel Forest Park protects some 72,000 hectares of the Coromandel Ranges. The most popular entrance to the park is the Kauaeranga Valley, where trampers can enjoy a walk to Pinnacles Hut and across landscapes with many well-preserved remnants of the kauri logging days.

However, the biggest attraction of the Coromandel landscape remains the idyllic, largely undeveloped beaches on the northern and eastern part of the peninsula, many of which still provide for the classic Kiwi camping holiday. One of the most popular short walks on the Coromandel Coast is out to the attractive cliffs and rock stacks at Cathedral Cove near the holiday town of Hahei. Adjacent to the shoreline here is one of New Zealand's earliest marine reserves, an area set aside as a fully protected nature reserve of the sea.

Gannet colony, Muriwai Scenic Reserve, Auckland

Kitekite Falls, Waitakere Ranges, Auckland

The Four Sisters, Trounson Kauri Park, Northland

Tane Mahuta, Waipoua Forest Sanctuary, Northland

Evening light, Hokianga Harbour, Northland

Sand patterns, Te Paki Recreation Reserve, Northland
OPPOSITE Sand dunes, Te Paki Recreation Reserve, Northland

Cape Reinga Lighthouse, Northland